ESS

PASTA

101 ESSENTIAL TIPS

PASTA

CONTRIBUTING EDITOR
Anne Willan

FENN

A Dorling Kindersley Book

Editor Irene Lyford
Art Editor Louise Bruce
Managing Editor Mary-Clare Jerram
Managing Art Editor Amanda Lunn
Production Controller Meryl Silbert
US Editor Ray Rogers

First published in Canada in 1995 by
Fenn Publishing Company Ltd.
1090 Lorimar Drive, Mississauga, Ontario L5S 1R8

ISBN 1-55168-028-9

Computer page makeup by Mark Bracey
Text film output by The Right Type, Great Britain
Reproduced by Colourscan, Singapore
Printed and bound by Graphicom, Italy

101 ESSENTIAL TIPS

PAGES 53-67

Filled & Baked Pasta

PAGES 68-69

Store & Reheat Pasta

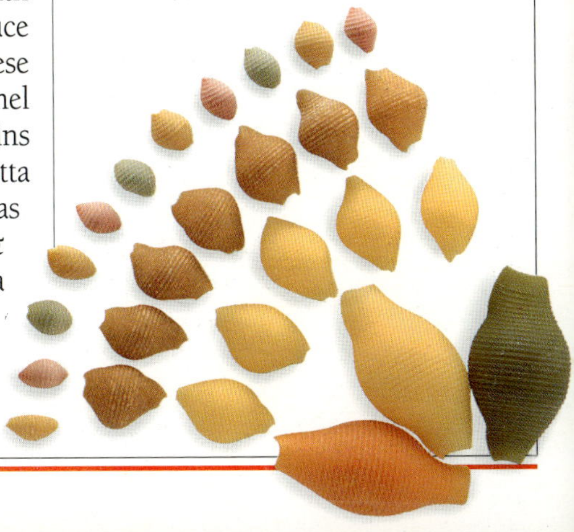

WHICH PASTA?

1 CALORIE COUNT

Pasta is an excellent source of carbohydrates, yet it is surprisingly low in calories. Protein and fiber content varies according to whether the pasta is made with or without eggs and which type of flour is used.

Typical analysis – cooked pasta

1oz (28g)	**Cal**	**Fiber**
Plain spaghetti	38	0.3g
Whole-wheat spaghetti	30	0.9g
Tagliatelle (egg pasta)	41	0.3g
Tagliatelle verde	37	0.3g

2 CHOOSING DRIED OR FRESH PASTA

Dried, commercially made pasta is an essential cupboard standby, providing the basis for a quick, cheap, and nutritious meal. Fresh, homemade egg pasta is deliciously light and inexpensive, but does take time to prepare. Store-bought fresh pasta, served with a simple home-made sauce, provides a fast, elegant, but more expensive, alternative.

3 BUY FRESH PASTA

Commercially made fresh egg pasta is widely available in a variety of shapes, colors, and flavors as well as in filled forms such as tortellini and ravioli. If possible, buy fresh pasta from a specialty store or a reputable retailer, check the information on packages, and avoid any nearing their "sell-by" date.

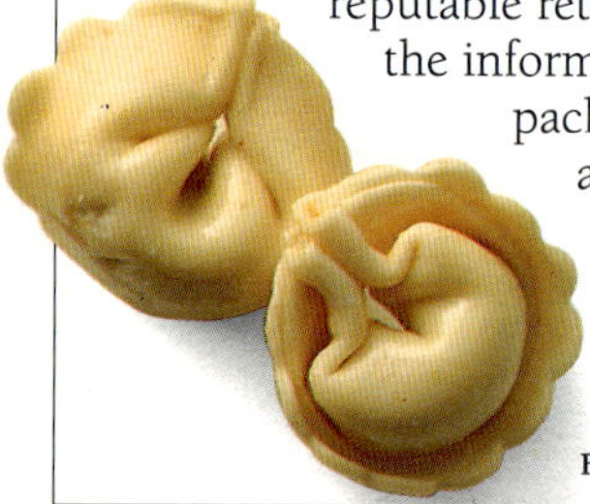

FILLED PASTA

4 DRIED PASTA CHOICE

Look for commercially produced dried pasta made from 100% pure durum wheat or semolina. Choose a whole-wheat variety for higher fiber content, or "*verde*" for the spinach-flavored version. Avoid packages with dusty crumbs in the bottom: this may indicate that the pasta is stale.

FARFALLE

5 LONG PASTA

There are two basic forms of long pasta: string shapes, such as spaghetti, and ribbons, such as tagliatelle. Commercially made string shapes are based on a simple flour and water paste, whereas ribbons often contain egg.

All are available fresh or dried and come in a range of sizes and in a variety of flavors, such as spinach, tomato, or whole-wheat. Ribbons are the most popular homemade pasta, since they are the easiest shape to cut, either by hand or machine.

CAPPELLINI

PAPPARDELLE

TAGLIATELLE VERDE

TAGLIARINI

SPAGHETTI

BUCKWHEAT SPAGHETTI

WHOLE-WHEAT SPAGHETTI

6 SHORT PASTA SHAPES

This group consists of a huge variety of shapes: tubes, shells, spirals, bows, rings, and wheels. Most of these shapes are commercially produced, dried pasta, made of flour and water paste, and are often available in different flavors or colors. Each shape has its own Italian name, which usually describes the object it resembles: for example, conchiglie (shell); farfalle (butterfly); lumache (snail); and ruoti (wheel).

TUBETTI LUNGHI

FARFALLE

CHIFFERI RIGATI

CAPPELLETTI

RIGATONI

RUOTI

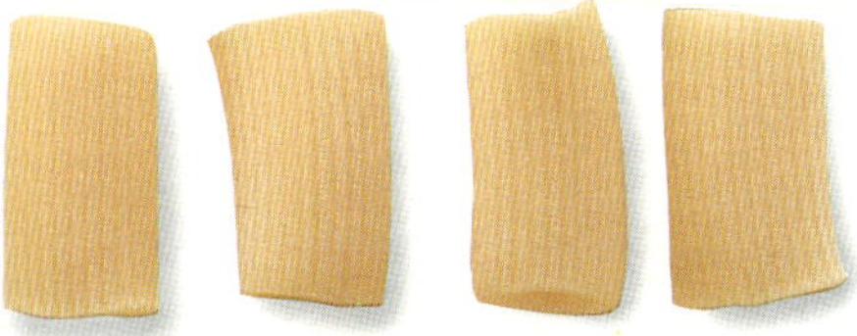

MILLERIGHE

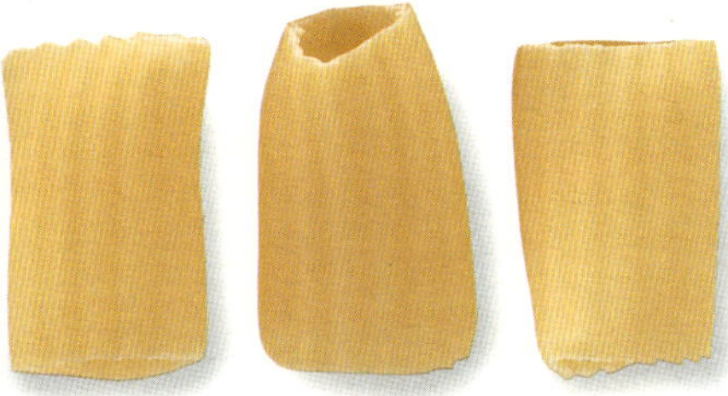

GIGANTONI

DITALINI

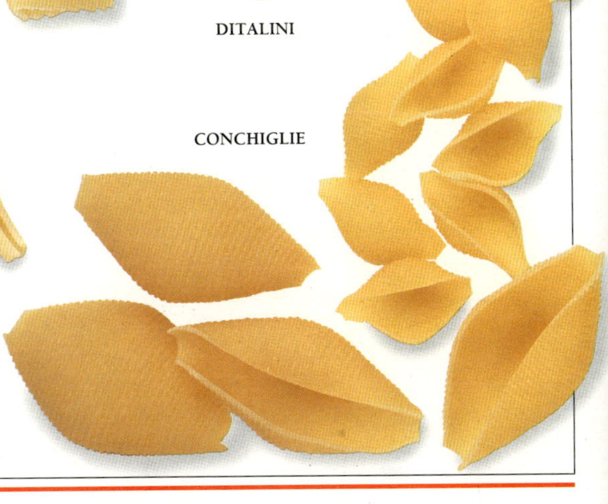

CONCHIGLIE

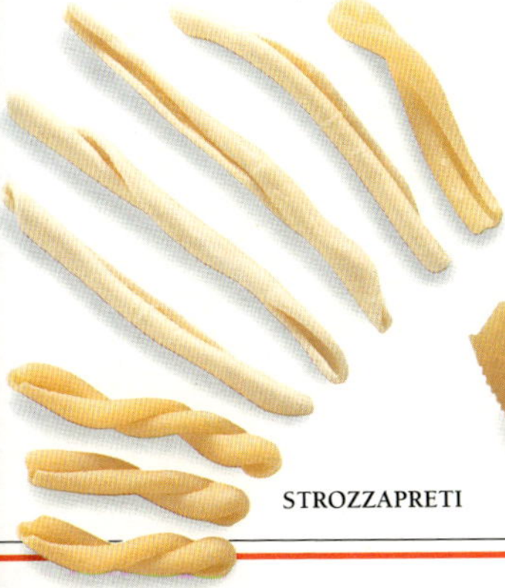

STROZZAPRETI

7 FILLED & LAYERED

Small pasta shapes, such as tortelloni, are filled with savory fillings, while in layered dishes, sheets of pasta (lasagne) are alternated with sauce and filling. For cannelloni, pasta rectangles are rolled up with a filling inside, topped with a sauce, and baked.

CANNELLONI

LASAGNE VERDE

LASAGNE

RIDGED LASAGNE VERDE

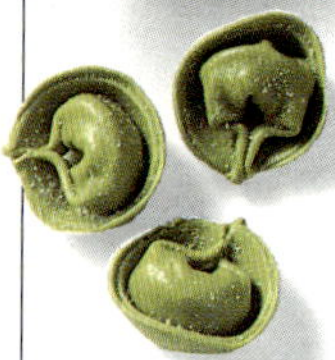

TORTELLONI VERDE

RAVIOLI

8 LITTLE PASTA FOR SOUP

Pastina–literally "little pasta"–is made in an immense variety of attractive and amusing shapes. Use pastina in light broths and simple children's dishes.

DITALINI

ORZO

ALPHABETTI

STELLINI

9 ORIENTAL PASTA

Many oriental noodles can be cooked in the same way as Italian pasta, but cellophane noodles and rice sticks are soaked before use. Crispy wontons and some mung-bean-starch noodles, are deep-fried.

CHINESE NOODLES

FINE DRIED EGG NOODLES

DRIED EGG NOODLES

FRESH NOODLES

10 MATCH SAUCE TO PASTA

Each pasta shape is suited to a particular type of sauce: homemade ribbons absorb butter- and cream-based sauces particularly well, while string shapes are best with sauces that cling – for example, those based on olive oil. Short pasta shapes are ideal with chunky sauces that get caught up in the folds and hollows, while small filled pastas require sauces that complement the filling without overwhelming it.

SPAGHETTI
Bolognese sauce clings well to long strands of spaghetti.

FUSILLI AL PESTO
Pesto, a classic basil sauce, suits long and short pasta.

SPINACH-CHEESE ROLLS
The red-pepper sauce adds a striking counterpoint.

CUPBOARD BASICS

11 WHICH FLOUR?

To make homemade egg pasta, use unbleached all-purpose flour. Semolina flour is not suitable for homemade pasta since it is hard to roll by hand. For extra fiber, you can use equal amounts of whole-wheat and white flour.

UNBLEACHED FLOUR

12 EGGS

Use the freshest eggs possible for homemade pasta. Immerse in water to test freshness: a newly laid egg will float on its side. Store eggs in the refrigerator but, for pasta dough, bring to room temperature before use.

NEWLY LAID EGG

13 OLIVE OIL

Olive oil is a natural partner for pasta dishes – whether served as a condiment or used in marinades and sauces. Choose unrefined oil from the first cold pressing of the olives. "Extra-virgin" describes the best European oil.

TOP-QUALITY OLIVE OIL

14 HERBS

Fresh herbs have the best flavor. If buying dried herbs, look for whole rather than chopped leaves. Use dried herbs sparingly: they have a stronger taste than fresh herbs.

PARSLEY
Parsley provides both flavor and garnish.

BASIL
The peppery flavor of basil is well suited to tomato-based dishes.

SAGE
Enhance pasta sauces with the subtle flavor of finely chopped fresh sage leaves.

THYME
Use fresh or dried sprigs or dried leaves for pungent seasoning. If using sprigs, remove before serving.

OREGANO ▷
With a peppery taste that is retained well in the dried form, oregano is often used to flavor pasta sauces, as well as other Italian dishes.

◁ MARJORAM
Marjoram is related to oregano but has a more delicate aroma. This herb is best used fresh.

15 SPICES

Buy whole spices, store them in well-sealed containers, and grind only when required. Try to select spices that complement the main dish ingredients.

JUNIPER BERRIES
Use fresh or dried to flavor meat or vegetable dishes.

NUTMEG
A little freshly grated nutmeg contributes a distinctive flavor to milk-based sauces.

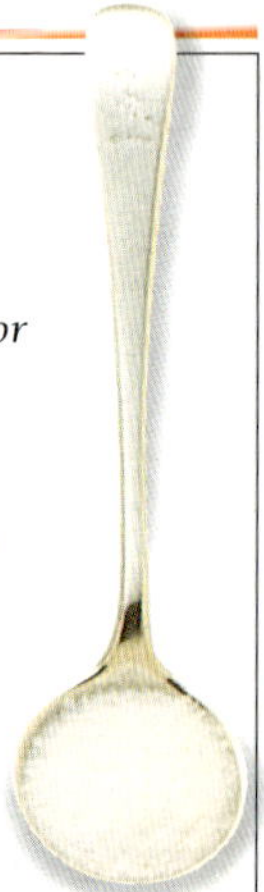

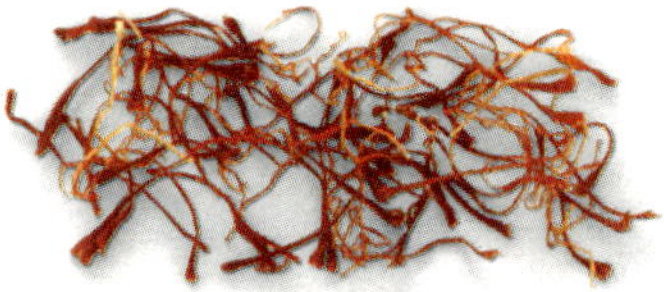

BLACK PEPPER
Black pepper is more pungent than white.

SAFFRON
Saffron, usually available as whole strands, provides color and flavor.

SALT
Add salt with caution, using your own taste to decide on the right amount.

16 GARLIC & ONIONS

Garlic and onions vary in flavor according to variety: red-skinned garlic and the common yellow onion are the strongest tasting. Fry garlic gently since it burns easily and becomes acrid.

△ **GARLIC**
Buy fresh, firm heads of garlic.

▽ **ONION**
Choose firm, dry bulbs with no black or powdery spots.

17 TOMATOES

The tomato, either fresh or in one of its many preserved forms, is often a vital ingredient in pasta recipes. Outdoor-grown, sun-ripened tomatoes have the best flavor of all.

COMMON TOMATO
Serve raw in salads and as a garnish, or peel, seed, and chop for soups and sauces.

PLUM TOMATO
Plum tomatoes have few seeds and excellent flavor.

CHERRY TOMATOES
Serve these tiny, flavor-packed tomatoes whole for a colorful pasta garnish.

TOMATO PUREE IN A TUBE
A tube of tomato puree is useful: it can be resealed after using a small amount.

SUN-DRIED TOMATOES
Available dried or stored in oil, a small quantity adds a distinctive flavor.

CHOPPED CANNED TOMATOES
Press through a sieve with a spoon for passata sauce.

WHOLE CANNED TOMATOES
The best plum tomatoes are from San Marzano, Italy.

CANNED TOMATO PUREE
For the best flavor, use double-concentrated puree.

18 OLIVES & CAPERS

For a simple pasta sauce, mix pureed olives with a little oil. Slightly more elaborate is a sauce that combines anchovies, olives, and capers *(see p.45)*.

GREEN OLIVES

CAPERS
Add capers toward the end of cooking time since heat intensifies their flavor and saltiness.

VINEGAR-PACKED CAPERS

SALTED CAPERS

OLIVES
Olives that are packed in oil or vinegar can be kept at room temperature, but refrigerate canned olives after opening.

BLACK OLIVES

19 SPINACH

Frozen chopped spinach is a useful cupboard standby; use it to color and flavor homemade pasta dough for pasta verde, or mix with ricotta cheese for a delicious filling. Whether you use fresh or frozen spinach, you must squeeze it thoroughly to remove all excess moisture after cooking and draining.

20 PINE NUTS

Toast pine nuts to enhance their sweet flavor. Use them whole or ground as in pesto, the well-known Italian basil-based sauce.

BLANCHED PINE NUTS

21 BALSAMIC VINEGAR

True balsamic vinegar, which is aged for several years, is very expensive. For use in sauces and salads, look for a cheaper, younger version with a rich flavor.

BALSAMIC VINEGAR

22 HAM & BACON

Many pasta recipes call for a quantity of ham or bacon. This is often diced or cut into thin strips and sauteed to add flavor and texture to sauces. Parma prosciutto is one of several fine Italian hams.

Pancetta is another regional Italian specialty – a type of bacon that is cured like ham. If you cannot find Pancetta, use good-quality lean smoked bacon instead.

23 CHEESES FOR PASTA

When buying hard cheeses such as Parmesan, ask for a piece to be cut from the whole cheese rather than choosing a precut piece sealed in plastic. Wrap the cheese in foil and keep it in the refrigerator. Keep fresh and soft cheeses in the refrigerator in an airtight container.

◁ MOZZARELLA
This creamy, mild cheese melts well for a pasta topping. Keep refrigerated in brine, 2–3 days.

△ PECORINO ROMANO
A hard cheese, made from sheep's milk, this is similar to Parmesan but has a sharper flavor.

△ RICOTTA
Frequently used as the basis for pasta fillings, ricotta is a delicate, creamy fresh cheese.

△ FONTINA
A semihard cheese with a smoky taste, fontina melts easily in sauces.

△ GORGONZOLA
An Italian blue cheese with a sharp flavor.

△ MASCARPONE
A fresh, dense dessert cheese.

PARMIGIANO △ REGGIANO
A hard, grainy cheese, this is the correct name for Parmesan cheese.

HOW TO MAKE FRESH PASTA

24 FRESH EGG PASTA DOUGH

Makes 1 lb (500 g)

Ingredients

2½ cups (300 g) flour
3 eggs
1 tbsp oil

1 ▷ Mound sifted flour on surface; add eggs, oil, and a pinch of salt.

2 ▷ With fingertips, combine eggs, oil, and salt. Gradually work in flour to form dough; add more flour if sticky.

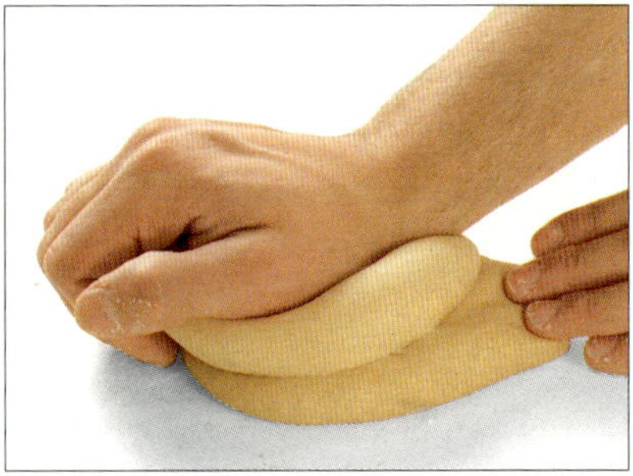

3 Scrape dough from work surface and form into ball; on floured surface, knead dough until elastic and smooth.

4 Form dough into ball and cover with bowl. Allow to rest for one hour at room temperature before rolling out.

25 MACHINE-MIX

Put flour, oil, and salt *(see p.20 for quantities)* into processor; add eggs one at a time, pulsing briefly between each. Process until dough is well mixed; form into ball.

ADD EGGS TO FLOUR

26 ADD FLAVORS

For pasta verde, add 2½ cups (75 g) spinach, cooked, drained, squeezed dry, and chopped, per egg. For tomato-flavored pasta, add 1 tablespoon puree per egg. Add flavorings along with the eggs.

PASTA VERDE

ADD SPINACH WITH EGGS

27 COLOR PASTA DOUGH

Add the ingredients suggested below to color your pasta dough (they have little effect on taste). You may need to add more flour to absorb the extra moisture.

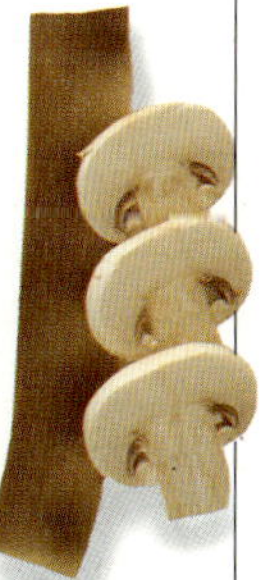

SAFFRON
For a warm, golden-colored dough, add a large pinch of saffron powder with the eggs.

BEET
Color pasta dough pink with 1 tablespoon of pureed, cooked beet per egg.

BASIL
Finely chop 2 tbsp fresh basil leaves. Work into the flour with the eggs.

MUSHROOM
Lightly cook ½ lb mushrooms; drain well and puree; add to flour with eggs.

28 Traditional rolling pin

Italian pasta cooks use a long rolling pin with no handles. The extra length is useful since the dough covers a large area when rolled out.

▽ Rolling by Hand
This traditional pasta pin is 32 in (80 cm) long.

29 Roll pasta dough by hand

Remove dough from under upturned bowl. Before beginning to roll, knead dough briefly on floured surface to work back any moisture that has appeared on the surface. Form into a ball with your hands.

1 Sprinkle surface with flour. Place ball of dough on work surface and flatten it slightly with rolling pin. Begin rolling out dough, turning and moving it all the time to prevent it from sticking.

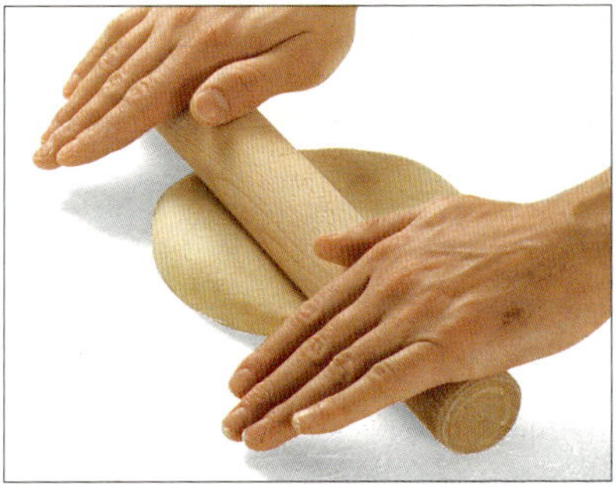

2 Continue rolling, pressing dough away from you, not pushing down, and always rolling in just one direction. Sprinkle work surface and rolling pin generously with flour as you work.

3 Keeping even pressure on rolling pin, carry on rolling until dough is almost transparent. If rolling pin is not long enough, divide dough into three and roll each piece separately. Keep other pieces wrapped in plastic.

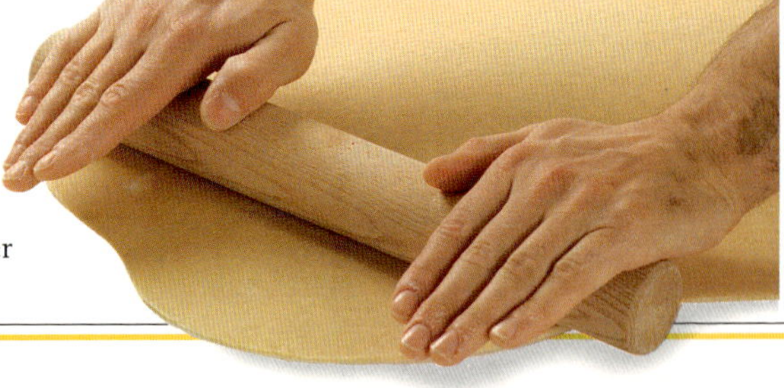

30 MACHINE-ROLL

A pasta machine gradually kneads the dough as it is rolled; it is not necessary to knead by hand.

1 Divide dough into three or four pieces and dust lightly with flour. Set machine rollers to widest setting and feed through one piece of dough.

2 Fold strip into thirds or quarters to form square; feed through machine again. Repeat folding and rolling seven to ten times until dough is smooth.

3 Tighten rollers one notch and feed dough through again. Continue rolling, tightening rollers one notch at a time, and ending with narrowest setting. Dust with flour if dough becomes sticky. Repeat with remaining pieces.

31 DRYING PASTA

When the pasta dough has been rolled out as thinly as possible, hang the pieces over a broom handle suspended between two chairs, or over the edge of a work surface. Allow the pasta to dry until it acquires a leathery look, 5–10 minutes, before cutting into the desired shapes.

DRY PASTA

How to Cut & Fill Pasta

32 Machine-cut

Only machine-rolled pasta can be cut by machine. Attach the cutters and select the required width setting. Pass each strip of dough through the machine.

Dry Pasta
Allow pasta to dry for 1–2 hours after cutting.

33 Useful cutters

A pastry wheel is perfect for cutting and sealing filled pasta and for cutting ribbons, whereas cookie cutters are ideal for cutting out pasta circles for filling. A sharp chef's knife is also useful.

COOKIE CUTTERS

PASTRY WHEEL

CHEF'S KNIFE

34 Cutting ribbons by hand

Sprinkle the rolled-out dough with flour, then roll it up loosely. With a sharp knife, cut across into ribbons of the required width: fettuccine, for example, is about ¼ in wide.

Carefully unravel the ribbons and sprinkle with flour. Lay them flat or loosely coiled on a floured towel, and allow to dry for 1–2 hours.

CUT RIBBONS TO DESIRED WIDTH

35 CUT FLAT SHEETS

When the rolled-out dough has dried a little, cut it with a long, sharp knife. For cannelloni, cut into 3 x 6 in (7.5 x 15 cm) rectangles. For lasagne, cut into pieces 2 in (5cm) wide and long enough to fit your dish. Sprinkle with flour and allow to dry for 1–2 hours.

CUT DOUGH ON FLOURED BOARD

36 PIPE PASTA FILLINGS

Spoon filling into a piping bag and push down to exclude any air. Twist end and hold tightly in one hand then, with the other hand, squeeze gently at the top of the bag to start the filling flowing.

GENTLY SQUEEZE BAG

37 FOLDED-FILLED PASTA

For folded-filled pasta, roll the dough out as thinly as possible. Place the filling in the center of each disk or square, fold over, and pinch the edges to seal. Allow to dry for 1–2 hours.

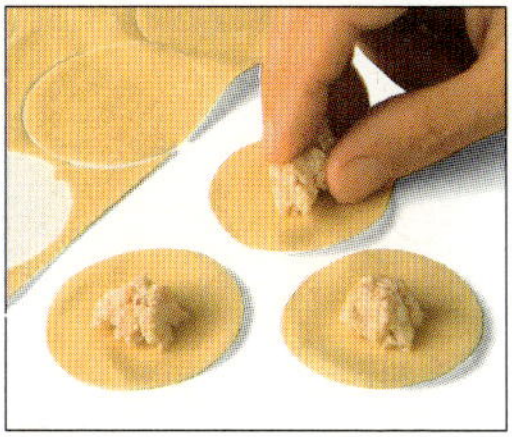

1 For tortellini, cut 2 in (5cm) disks from pasta dough. Place some filling in center of each disk.

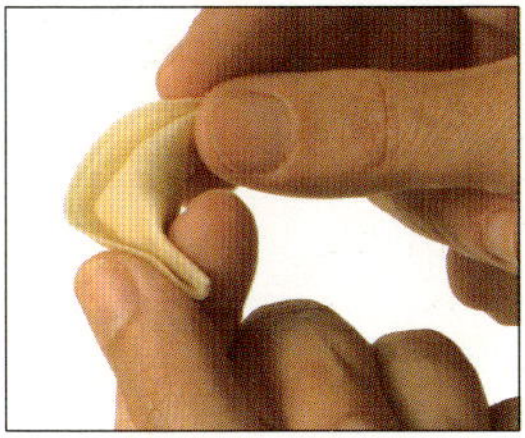

2 Wet edge of disk; fold in half and seal edges. Curve around finger then pinch ends together.

PANSOTI AND CAPPELLETTI
Both are simple folded-filled squares, but cappelletti are also curved into a hat shape.

38 SANDWICH-FILLED PASTA

In this form of filled pasta, the filling is sandwiched between two layers of dough, which are then cut into squares or circles. Roll the pasta as thinly as possible – not more than $1/16$ in (1.5 mm) thick.

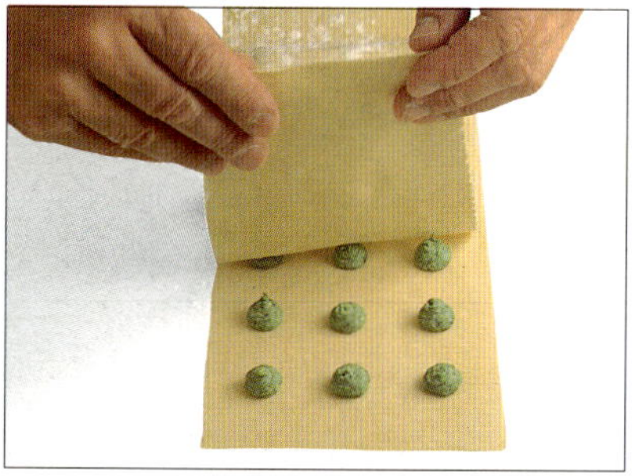

1 Cut pasta into two equal rectangles. Moisten surface of one sheet with water. Pipe small mounds of filling on the dough, spaced 1½ in (4 cm) apart.

2 Lay second rectangle on top. Press floured piping tube over mounds to seal dough around filling. Press around mounds with fingers to seal layers.

3 With fluted pastry wheel or large chef's knife, cut between mounds to separate rectangle into equal-sized squares. Place on towel to dry.

FRESH, FILLED PASTA
After allowing to dry for 1–2 hours, cook fresh, filled pasta immediately, or store in the refrigerator and cook within one day.

COOK & SERVE PASTA

39 PASTA PORTIONS

1 lb (500 g) fresh or dried pasta will serve six to eight as an appetizer, or four as a main course; use less pasta if the sauce is rich.

Filled or layered pasta made with store-bought, dried pasta is heavier than fresh filled pasta, so serve smaller portions. The same applies to whole-wheat pasta, which is more filling than the white-flour variety.

40 SAUCEPAN SIZE

Use a pan that is big enough to contain sufficient water for the quantity of pasta to be cooked, and to leave enough room for the pasta pieces to move around freely in the water without touching and sticking together.

CHOICE OF PAN SIZES

41 PASTA-TO-WATER

Add salt to taste

Pasta	Water
½ lb (250 g)	2½ quarts (3 liters)
1 lb (500 g)	4 quarts (5 liters)
1½ lb (750 g)	5 quarts (6 liters)

42 FAST-BOIL PASTA

Pasta must be cooked in fast-boiling water. Bring the water to a boil before adding the pasta; cover the pot until the water comes back to a boil, then remove the lid.

STIR PASTA TO PREVENT STICKING

43 ADD PASTA TO WATER

When the water is boiling, add salt as required, then add pasta. Stir immediately to prevent the pasta from sticking to the pot or to itself and to ensure that it is totally immersed.

◁ LONG PASTA
Allow long sticks of pasta to curl into the water as they soften; do not break them.

HOMEMADE PASTA ▷
Drop homemade pasta straight into a pan of boiling water from the towel on which it was drying.

44 PASTA DRAINER

Cook small or finely cut pasta in a pasta drainer immersed in a pan of boiling water. When the pasta is cooked, simply lift out and drain.

COOKING SMALL PASTA IN A DRAINER

45 IS IT READY?

Cook pasta until it is slightly resistant when nipped with a thumbnail, or firm to the bite *(al dente)*, with no hard center or raw taste.

TEST WITH THUMBNAIL

46 DRAIN & RINSE

As soon as the pasta is ready, drain and rinse – in hot water if it is to be served hot, in cold if it is to be used in a salad or in a baked dish.

DRAIN IN COLANDER

47 SERVE HOT

Pasta cools down rapidly, so warm the serving bowl or individual plates, and serve the pasta as soon as it is cooked and drained.

SERVE IN WARM BOWL

48 TOSS QUICKLY

Toss hot, cooked pasta with the prepared sauce or dressing as soon as the pasta is ready. If left to stand, pasta tends to stick together.

COAT WITH SAUCE

49 PAN-FRY PASTA

Pan-fry uncooked fresh egg pasta (particularly string shapes) in hot oil to make a crisp brown cake, and serve with sauce. Alternatively, mix cooked pasta with egg and pan-fry it as you would a pancake.

50 DEEP-FRYING

Filled oriental pasta, such as wontons and egg rolls, are usually deep-fried. You can use the same technique for stuffed, Italian-style pasta such as cannelloni or ravioli. Cook these in batches until golden brown, then drain on paper towels.

51 PREVENT STICKING

Pasta has a tendency to stick to the sides of the dish when baked. To prevent this, brush the dish with a little oil or melted butter. If the recipe includes a sauce, coat the sides of the dish with it before adding the pasta.

OIL BAKING DISH

52 AVOID A CRUST

To prevent pasta from drying out and becoming too crusty when baked, spread a thick layer of sauce on top, making sure that all of the pasta is well covered. Alternatively, cover the top of the baking dish with a sheet of aluminum foil.

SAUCE TOPPING *Here, a top layer of tomato-cream sauce will help prevent the pasta from drying out.*

53 PERFECT PARTNERS

Parmigiano-Reggiano cheese, more commonly known as Parmesan, is the perfect complement to many pasta dishes. Use it to flavor sauces or fillings, or sprinkle it on top of cooked pasta. Although Parmesan is expensive, a little goes a long way.

FRESH IS BEST *Freshly grated Parmesan is far superior to the pregrated variety in tubs and cans.*

54 GARNISHES

Choose a garnish to complement the taste and enhance the appearance of a dish. Typical garnishes for pasta dishes include basil and parsley (chopped or sprigs), curls of Parmesan cheese, olives, capers, and mussels or clams.

SLICED OLIVES

PARSLEY

BASIL

CHERRY TOMATOES

◁ COMPLEMENTARY GARNISHES
The garnish of finely grated lemon zest echoes the dish's lemon sauce, while the green scallion rings provide an attractive color contrast.

55 HOW TO EAT LONG PASTA

It is possible to eat long pasta elegantly if you follow this very simple technique:

- Pick up a few strands on the prongs of a fork.
- Hold the tip of the fork firmly against the side of the bowl, or in the hollow of a spoon held in the other hand.
- Twirl the fork around until the strands are all rolled onto it.

TWIRL SPAGHETTI ONTO FORK

PASTA SOUPS & SALADS

56 MINESTRONE SOUP

Serves 6–8 as appetizer or light lunch

Ingredients

⅔ cup (110 g) great northern beans, soaked
2 carrots, diced
2 onions, diced
4 stalks celery, sliced
¼ cup (60 ml) olive oil
3 quarts (3 liters) chicken or vegetable stock
1 bay leaf
2 leeks, sliced
12 green beans, cut in ½ in (1.25 cm) pieces
1 garlic clove, crushed
Salt and pepper
1 small cauliflower, divided into florets
1 cup (90 g) ditalini
2 zucchini, cut in ½ in (1.25 cm) pieces
3 tomatoes, peeled, seeded, and chopped
1 cup (30 g) chopped fresh basil or parsley
1⅓ cups (110 g) grated Parmesan cheese

- Simmer white beans until quite tender, approximately 2 hours. Take off heat and leave in liquid.
- Sauté diced carrots, onions, and celery in olive oil. Add chicken or vegetable stock, bay leaf, and white beans in their liquid, and bring to boil. Add sliced leeks, green beans, garlic, salt and pepper. Cover and simmer for 5 minutes. Add cauliflower florets and ditalini and cook until pasta is *al dente*, about 10 minutes. Add zucchini and tomatoes and simmer until tender, 5 minutes.
- Remove bay leaf; stir in chopped basil or parsley. Serve with Parmesan cheese.

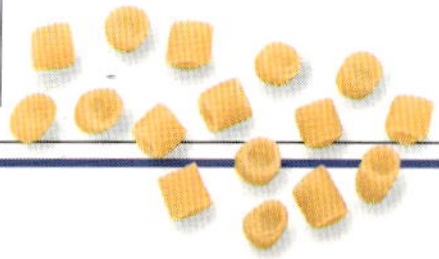

57 VEGETABLE NOODLE SOUP

Serves 6–8 as appetizer or light lunch

Ingredients

4 medium leeks
2 cups (175 g) turnips, diced
4 carrots, diced
3 celery stalks, diced
½ head white cabbage, finely shredded
¾ cup (125 g) green beans, sliced
2 garlic cloves, chopped
2½ quarts (2.5 liters) chicken stock
Bouquet garni
Salt and pepper
2 small zucchini, diced
1 large tomato, peeled, seeded, and chopped
¼ lb (125 g) vermicelli

- Trim leeks; slit each in half lengthwise, then wash thoroughly under cold running water to get rid of any dirt. With sharp knife, cut each leek half crosswise into ¼ in (5 mm) slices.
- Put leeks, turnips, carrots, celery, cabbage, beans, and chopped garlic into large stockpot.
- Add chicken stock, bouquet garni, and salt and pepper. Bring to boil; cover, and simmer for 30 minutes. Add zucchini and tomatoes and simmer until tender, about 25 minutes longer.
- Stir in vermicelli and continue simmering until pasta is just tender, 4–5 minutes.

TO SERVE
The soup is served here with tomato-flavored croûtes.

58 FUSILLI & PESTO SALAD

Serves 6–8 as appetizer

Ingredients

2 cups (60 g) fresh basil
6 garlic cloves
6 tbsp pine nuts
1⅓ cups (125 g) Parmesan
¾ cup (175 ml) olive oil
Salt and pepper
1 lb (500 g) fusilli

1 Strip off basil leaves from stalks, reserving a few sprigs for garnish; rinse and pat dry. Put in processor with garlic, nuts, and Parmesan.

2 Add 3 tbsp olive oil and process until smooth, scraping down bowl as necessary.

TO SERVE

Spoon the sauce-coated fusilli onto individual plates and garnish with the reserved sprigs of basil. Here, cherry tomatoes add bright contrast.

3 With blade turning, add remaining oil, pouring it in slowly so sauce emulsifies. When all oil has been added, scrape down sides of bowl and process again briefly. Season to taste with salt and pepper and transfer to mixing bowl. Cook fusilli in boiling salted water until *al dente*. Drain.

4 Rinse drained fusilli under cold running water. Drain thoroughly. Add to sauce in mixing bowl and toss together until pasta is well coated.

59 HOT PARSLEY PASTA SALAD

Serves 6 as appetizer

Ingredients

Pasta dough
2 cups (225 g) flour
2 eggs and 1 egg yolk
2 tbsp water
1 tsp salt

Medium bunch of flat-leaf parsley
Sprigs of flat parsley, chopped
4 tsp red wine vinegar
2½ tbsp sour cream
1 garlic clove, chopped
2 shallots, chopped
Salt and pepper
¼ cup vegetable oil
2 hard-boiled eggs, shelled and sliced

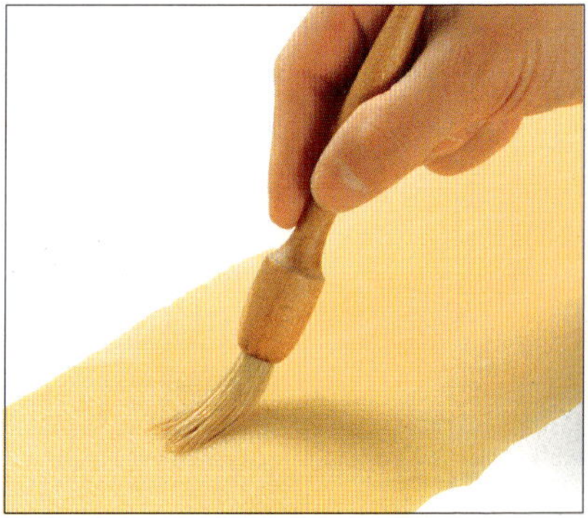

1 Make pasta dough (*see p.20*), omitting oil and adding egg yolk and water in place of one egg. Knead until smooth and elastic. Roll into 5 in (13 cm) strips. Brush water over half of each pasta strip.

2 Pull leaves off parsley. Arrange leaves in rows about 1 in (2.5 cm) apart on dampened half of dough strip; fold other half over. Roll gently with rolling pin to seal layers together. Repeat process with remaining strips of fresh pasta dough.

3 With pastry wheel or chef's knife cut dough, between rows of parsley leaves, into 1 in (2.5 cm) squares. Place squares on floured towel and sprinkle lightly with flour. Allow to dry 1–2 hours.

4 Chop parsley sprigs, reserving few for garnish; whisk vinegar, cream, garlic, shallots, chopped parsley, salt and pepper until slightly thickened. Gradually add oil.

5 Cook pasta squares in boiling salted water until tender but still chewy. Drain; rinse with hot water; drain again. Add to dressing and toss gently to mix.

TO SERVE
Garnish with a slice of hard-boiled egg and a sprig of parsley.

60 Fresh Tuna Pasta Salad Niçoise

Serves 6 as main course

Ingredients

Marinade and dressing
8 anchovy fillets, chopped
1 sprig of fresh thyme, chopped
2 garlic cloves, chopped
¼ cup (60 ml) lemon juice
1 tbsp balsamic vinegar
1 tsp Dijon mustard
Black pepper
1 cup (250 ml) olive oil

2 lb (1 kg) fresh tuna steaks, skinned and cut into 1 in (2.5 cm) cubes
1½ lb (750 g) green beans
1 lb (500 g) farfalle
1 lb (500 g) cherry tomatoes
1 cup (100g) pitted black olives

1 Make marinade: put anchovies, thyme, and garlic in bowl and mix. Add lemon juice, vinegar, mustard, and black pepper and whisk together. Slowly add olive oil, whisking until mixture emulsifies.

2 ▽ Thread tuna cubes onto skewers and place on large plate. Spoon about 5 tablespoons of marinade over kebabs and cover with plastic. Allow to marinate in refrigerator for at least 1 hour, turning skewers occasionally.

3 △ Trim the green beans. Rinse, then cook in boiling salted water until tender but still firm. Drain beans, rinse under cold running water, and drain. Place in bowl with 5 tablespoons of dressing.

4 Toss green beans with dressing; set aside. Cook farfalle. Drain well; rinse under cold water; drain. Put in bowl with 5 tablespoons of dressing; toss together.

5 Broil kebabs for 2 minutes; turn and baste with dressing, then broil for a further 2 minutes. Arrange on plates with farfalle, cherry tomatoes, and beans.

TO SERVE
Spoon the remaining dressing over each serving. If you wish, garnish with olives.

61 ASIAN NOODLE SALAD

Serves 4 as main course

Ingredients

Spicy soy dressing
¾ in (2 cm) piece of fresh ginger root
2 fresh green chilies
2 garlic cloves, peeled and chopped
2 tsp sugar
¼ cup (60 ml) rice wine vinegar
½ cup (125 ml) soy sauce
¼ cup (60 ml) peanut oil
2 tbsp sesame oil

½ lb (225 g) fine dried egg noodles
2¼ cups (175 g) snow peas, trimmed
4 scallions
⅔ cup (75 g) roasted unsalted peanuts
Small bunch fresh cilantro
¾ lb (375 g) cooked peeled shrimp
Salt and pepper

- Prepare dressing: peel, slice, and crush ginger root. Core, seed, and dice chilies. Put in bowl with garlic, sugar, and vinegar. Stir in soy sauce. Add peanut and sesame oil and whisk until sauce emulsifies and thickens. Check seasoning.
- Cook egg noodles in boiling salted water till tender but still chewy, 4–6 minutes, stirring occasionally. Drain noodles, rinse with hot water, and drain again thoroughly.
- Place noodles in large bowl; pour over dressing; toss until well coated. Set aside for at least 1 hour.
- Cook snow peas in boiling salted water until tender yet crisp, 2–3 minutes. Drain, rinse with running cold water, and drain again. Cut each pod diagonally into 2–3 slices.
- Cut scallions crosswise into thin diagonal slices, including some green tops. Coarsely chop peanuts. Strip cilantro leaves from stalks, and chop leaves coarsely.
- Add snow peas, scallions, two-thirds of peanuts and cilantro, and all shrimp to noodles. Toss together thoroughly. Season to taste.

TO SERVE

Garnish salad with remaining chopped peanuts and coarsely chopped cilantro.

Pasta Sauces

62 Classic Bechamel Sauce

Makes 1 cup (250 ml)

Ingredients

1 cup (250 ml) milk
4½ tsp butter
3 tbsp flour
Grated nutmeg
Salt and white pepper

Bring milk to boil in saucepan; set aside. In heavy saucepan, melt butter. Whisk in flour and cook until foaming, about 1 minute. Remove pan from heat and cool slightly. Strain milk through sieve and add to pan, whisking constantly. Return sauce to heat and bring to a boil, whisking until sauce thickens. Season to taste with nutmeg, salt and pepper, and simmer for another 2 minutes.

63 Fresh Tomato Sauce

Makes 1½ cups (375 ml)

Ingredients

3 tbsp vegetable oil
2 medium onions, finely chopped
2 lb (1 kg) tomatoes, chopped
3 garlic cloves, chopped
2 tbsp tomato puree
1 tsp sugar
Bouquet garni
Salt and pepper

1 In large pan heat oil; sauté onions till brown, stirring often. Add tomatoes, garlic, puree, sugar, and bouquet garni.

2 Cook tomato mixture until it is fairly thick, 12–15 minutes. Strain through strainer into bowl. Press down with small ladle to extract all tomato pulp. Season to taste with salt and pepper.

64 Pesto sauce

For 1 lb (500 g) pasta

Ingredients

1½ cups (45 g) basil leaves, washed, dried, and chopped
6 garlic cloves, peeled
⅓ cup (40 g) pine nuts
1⅓ cup (125 g) grated Parmesan cheese
¾ cup (175 ml) olive oil
Salt and pepper

1 Place chopped basil leaves, garlic, pine nuts, and Parmesan cheese in mortar. Pound with pestle to combine.

2 When basil and Parmesan mixture forms smooth puree, gradually add olive oil. Continue pounding until oil is incorporated and sauce is well blended.

3 Before serving Pesto sauce, season to taste with salt and pepper. (If you like, puree ingredients in food processor, adding olive oil with blade turning.)

65 Freeze pesto portions

Pesto freezes well, without any loss of flavor or color. Make double or triple quantities of recipe and freeze the extra in an ice-cube tray for single-serving portions. Toss a portion with hot spaghetti for a quick individual snack, or stir into vegetable soup for added flavor.

66 CARBONARA

For 1 lb (500 g) pasta

Ingredients

2 tbsp butter
2 garlic cloves, peeled and chopped
½ lb (225 g) sliced pancetta or smoked bacon, cut into strips
¼ cup (60 ml) dry white wine
4 eggs
1 cup (90 g) grated Parmesan cheese
Salt and pepper
Sprigs of parsley

▪ Melt butter in skillet; gently sauté garlic and sliced pancetta or bacon for 1–2 minutes. Add white wine and continue cooking till the liquid is reduced by half. Remove pan from heat and keep mixture warm.

FRESH BROWN EGGS

TO SERVE

Carbonara is served here with fettuccine, sprinkled with freshly ground black pepper.

▪ Put eggs and Parmesan cheese in large bowl. Season lightly with salt and pepper and beat well with fork. Finely chop sprigs of parsley.

▪ Add hot cooked pasta to egg and Parmesan mixture in bowl and toss quickly. Add pancetta mixture and chopped parsley. Toss together and serve immediately on warm plates.

67 SERVING CARBONARA SAUCE

The eggs in Carbonara sauce *(see above)* are not cooked, but just lightly set by the heat of the cooked pasta. It is essential, therefore, that the pasta is added as soon as it has been drained, rinsed with hot water, and drained again. Toss together, and serve immediately on hot plates.

68 Egg & anchovy

For 1 lb (500 g) pasta

Ingredients

4 anchovy fillets
¼ lb (125 g) mozzarella cheese
3 egg yolks
5 tbsp butter, cut into pieces

Chop anchovy fillets and mozzarella cheese. Lightly beat egg yolks and combine with anchovies and cheese in serving bowl. Toss with butter and hot cooked pasta of choice.

69 Gorgonzola

For 1 lb (500 g) pasta

Ingredients

¼ lb (125 g) Gorgonzola cheese
½ cup (125 ml) heavy cream
2 tbsp butter
⅓ cup (30 g) grated Parmesan cheese

Crumble Gorgonzola cheese into pan with heavy cream and butter; stir over low heat until smooth. Toss with freshly grated Parmesan cheese and hot cooked pasta.

70 Seafood sauce

For 1 lb (500 g) pasta

Ingredients

¼ cup (60 ml) olive oil
1 onion, chopped
1 carrot, chopped
2 garlic cloves, chopped
¼ lb (125 g) mushrooms, sliced
Salt and pepper
¼ cup (60 ml) dry white wine
2 plum tomatoes, peeled, seeded, and chopped
1 lb (500 g) shrimp, shelled
2 lb (1 kg) mussels or clams, steamed open and shelled; reserve cooking liquid
3 tbsp chopped parsley

▪ Heat olive oil in sauté pan and cook onion and carrot until soft. Add chopped garlic cloves, sliced mushrooms, and salt and pepper to taste. Mix ingredients together.

▪ Lower heat and cook until all liquid in pan has evaporated, 2–3 minutes. Pour in wine and cook for 4–5 minutes to reduce sauce. Add chopped tomatoes and simmer for another 5–7 minutes.

▪ Add shrimp and simmer for 1–2 minutes. Add mussels or clams with 1 cup (250 ml) of their cooking liquid, strained. Add chopped parsley, and check and adjust seasoning.

▪ Serve with spaghetti.

71 TOMATO & BASIL SAUCE

For 1 lb (500 g) pasta

Ingredients

Large bunch fresh basil
1 garlic clove
5 medium ripe tomatoes
½ cup (125 ml) extra-virgin olive oil
Salt and pepper

- Strip basil leaves from stalks and chop coarsely. Finely chop garlic. Chop tomatoes without peeling or seeding them.
- Place basil, garlic, and tomatoes in bowl and add olive oil. Stir to combine. Season to taste with salt and pepper. Serve with hot cooked fettuccine.

TO SERVE
Sprinkle freshly grated Parmesan cheese over Tomato & Basil Sauce, which is served here with fettuccine.

72 PUTTANESCA SAUCE

For 12 oz (375 g) pasta

Ingredients

3 garlic cloves
1 dried red chili pepper
6 anchovy fillets
1 lb (500 g) tomatoes
6 tbsp olive oil
⅔ cup (125 g) large black olives, pitted
1 tbsp capers
Salt

- Finely chop garlic; chop red chili pepper and anchovy fillets; peel, seed, and chop tomatoes.
- Heat oil in skillet and fry garlic and chili pepper until garlic starts to brown. Add chopped anchovy fillets and mash with fork.
- Add tomatoes, olives, and capers to mixture in skillet and stir well. Season to taste with salt. Continue simmering while pasta is cooking.
- Serve with hot, cooked spaghetti.

73 SPICY TOMATO & BACON

For 1 lb (500 g) pasta

Ingredients

3 lb (1.4 kg) plum tomatoes
1 fresh red chili pepper
¾ lb (375 g) mushrooms
5–7 sprigs fresh oregano
4 thick-cut slices bacon
2 garlic cloves
Salt and pepper

▪ Peel, seed, and chop tomatoes coarsely. Cut fresh red chili pepper lengthwise in half; remove core and fleshy white ribs and scrape out seeds; dice finely.

▪ Wipe mushrooms with dampened paper towels and trim stalks. Place mushrooms stalkside down and slice across. Strip oregano leaves from stalks, reserving few leaves for garnish; chop leaves finely. Stack bacon on cutting board and cut across into wide strips. Peel and finely chop garlic cloves.

▪ In skillet, fry bacon over low heat, stirring occasionally, until browned, 5–7 minutes. Spoon off fat, leaving about 3 tbsp in which to sauté sliced mushrooms. Increase heat; add mushrooms to skillet. Cook until mushrooms are softened and most of liquid has evaporated, stirring with wooden spoon to prevent sticking.

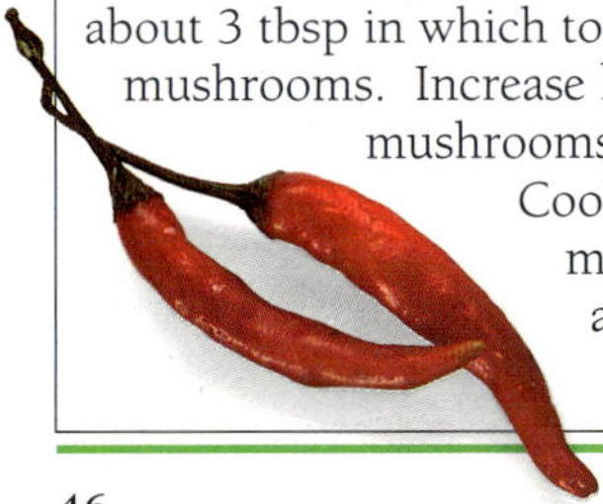

▪ Add chopped tomatoes with their juice to mushrooms in skillet, together with garlic, chili pepper, oregano, salt, and pepper. Bring to boil, cover with lid, and simmer, stirring occasionally until sauce is thick and rich, 25–30 minutes.

▪ If sauce needs thickening, cook without lid for a few minutes more.

▪ Check sauce for seasoning. Pour sauce over hot cooked pasta and toss together. If you like, sprinkle each serving with Parmesan cheese.

TO SERVE

Sprinkle freshly grated Parmesan cheese over each serving and garnish with oregano leaves.

74 PRIMAVERA SAUCE

For 1 lb (500 g) pasta

Ingredients

2 medium zucchini
Salt and pepper
2 medium carrots
2 cups (200 g) shelled peas
3 tbsp butter
¾ cup (175 ml) heavy cream
⅓ cup (30 g) grated Parmesan cheese

TO SERVE ▽
Primavera is served here with spaghetti and a baked zucchini fan garnish.

- Trim ends of zucchini and cut each in half lengthwise. Cut each half lengthwise in half again. Next, cut zucchini lengths into ⅜ in (9 mm) chunks. Simmer in boiling salted water until barely tender, 2–3 minutes. Drain in colander, rinse with cold water, then drain again thoroughly. Set zucchini aside until needed.
- Peel and trim ends of carrots; cut into chunks of a similar size to zucchini. Place in saucepan and cover with cold water; add salt, and bring to boil. Simmer until just tender, 8–10 minutes. Drain in colander, rinse with cold water, then drain thoroughly. Set carrots aside until needed.
- Bring small saucepan of salted water to boil. Add peas and simmer until tender, 3–8 minutes. Drain, rinse with cold water, and drain again thoroughly. Set peas aside until they are needed.
- Heat butter in large pan; add zucchini and carrot chunks and peas and sauté for 1 minute. Add cream, stir well to mix, and heat until mixture is simmering. Remove pan from heat, add cooked, drained pasta, and toss with cream and vegetable mixture. Add freshly grated Parmesan cheese and toss gently to combine.

75 RAGU BOLOGNESE

For 1 lb (500 g) pasta

Ingredients

4 tbsp vegetable oil
2 onions, chopped
2 garlic cloves, chopped
1 medium carrot, diced
¾ lb (375 g) ground beef
¾ lb (375 g) ground pork
1 cup (250 ml) milk
1½ cups (375 ml) dry white wine
2 lb (1 kg) tomatoes
1 tbsp tomato puree
Bouquet garni
Salt and pepper
2 cups (500 ml) water

TO SERVE △
Ragù Bolognese is served here with its classic partner, spaghetti, and sprinkled liberally with Parmesan cheese.

1 Heat vegetable oil in sauté pan, add chopped onions, chopped garlic, and diced carrot, and sauté until soft, stirring frequently. Add ground beef and ground pork and cook until they lose their pink color. Add milk, stir, then simmer until liquid has evaporated. Add white wine and simmer until it also has evaporated.

2 Peel, seed, and coarsely chop tomatoes. Add to meat mixture in sauté pan with any juice. Add tomato puree, bouquet garni, salt and pepper to taste, and water. Simmer until sauce is thick, 1½–2 hours, stirring occasionally. Add a little water if sauce starts to stick. Discard bouquet garni and check seasoning before serving.

76 ALFREDO SAUCE

For 500 g (1 lb) pasta

Ingredients

4 tbsp butter
1 cup (250 ml) heavy cream
⅔ cup (60 g) grated Parmesan cheese

TO SERVE
Serve with freshly ground black pepper and grated Parmesan cheese.

- In large pan, cook pasta of choice in boiling salted water; when ready, drain well and return to pan. Meanwhile, in small pan, melt butter, add heavy cream and bring almost to boil. Pour over hot, cooked pasta in large pan, and toss gently over low heat until pasta is coated with sauce.
- Add freshly grated Parmesan cheese to pasta mixture and continue tossing over low heat until mixture is very hot. Check and adjust seasoning.
- Serve at once on warmed plates.

77 WHITE CLAM SAUCE

For 1 lb (500 g) pasta

Ingredients

8 lb (3.6 kg) clams
1 onion, finely chopped
1 cup (250 ml) dry white wine
2 garlic cloves, finely chopped
¼ cup (60 ml) olive oil
Sprigs of parsley, chopped
Salt and pepper

TO SERVE
Garnish, as here, with clams in shells and sprigs of parsley.

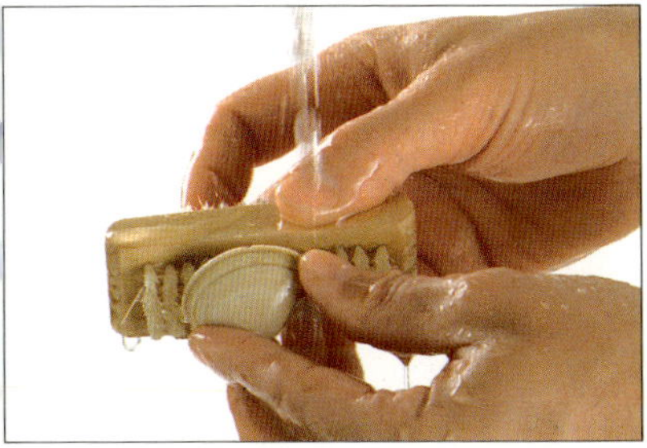

1 Scrub clams; put in large pan with onion and wine. Cook until shells open; discard any unopened clams.

2 Remove clams from pan, reserving liquid. When cool, take clams from shells; reserve a few in shells for garnish.

3 Reduce clam cooking liquid over high heat until only about 1 cup (250 ml) remains. Strain cooking liquid into small bowl through fine sieve. Sauté garlic in oil for 30 seconds, being careful not to burn; add shelled clams, chopped parsley, and reduced cooking liquid, and stir to mix. Season to taste with salt and pepper. Serve with spinach linguine. Garnish with a few clams in their shells.

78 RED CLAM SAUCE

For 1 lb (500 g) pasta

Ingredients

As for White Clam Sauce
2 lb (1kg) tomatoes

Follow Steps 1 and 2 of recipe for White Clam Sauce. Peel, seed, and chop tomatoes. Add at Step 3, after sautéing garlic. Simmer till mixture thickens, stirring occasionally. Add clams, cooking liquid, and parsley.

SERVE WITH SPINACH LINGUINE

79 Olive Oil & Garlic Dressing

For 1 lb (500 g) pasta

Ingredients

4 garlic cloves
½ cup (125 ml) olive oil
Salt and pepper

Finely chop garlic cloves. Heat garlic in olive oil until golden brown, being careful not to burn it. Season with salt and pepper. Serve with long, thin pasta such as cappellini or spaghettini.

80 Three Cheeses

For 1 lb (500 g) pasta

Ingredients

¼ lb (125 g) Gorgonzola cheese
¾ cup (175 ml) heavy cream
⅔ cup (60 g) freshly grated Parmesan cheese
½ cup (125 g) ricotta cheese

ADD RICOTTA CHEESE

To Serve
Toss sauce with fresh fettuccine.

Remove rind from Gorgonzola cheese; chop into fairly small pieces. Place in saucepan with cream, Parmesan cheese, and ricotta cheese. Heat gently, stirring all the time, until all three cheeses are melted. Be careful not to overheat sauce.

81 Choosing & Cooking Cheese

Hard cheeses such as Gruyère and Parmesan can withstand higher temperatures, so are a good choice for cooking. When adding grated cheese to a sauce, heat until just melted: never boil or reheat.

FILLED & BAKED PASTA

82 MEAT FILLING

For ¾ lb (375 g) pasta

Ingredients

3 tbsp butter
1 small onion, finely chopped
2 carrots, finely chopped
1 celery stalk, finely chopped
½ oz (15 g) dried mushrooms, soaked and chopped
1 lb (500 g) lean ground beef
½ cup (125 ml) Marsala
2 tbsp tomato puree

▪ Melt butter in skillet. Sauté onion, carrots, and celery until soft. Add mushrooms (reserving soaking liquid) and beef. Cook until minced beef loses pink color, 4–5 minutes.
▪ Add Marsala to meat mixture and boil until liquid has evaporated. Add tomato puree dissolved in some of mushroom soaking liquid. Stir and cover pan. Simmer for 1 hour, stirring occasionally. If mixture begins to stick, add a little water.
▪ Cool before using to fill small pasta shapes.

83 CHEESE FILLING

For ¾ lb (375 g) pasta

Ingredients

2 lb (1 kg) spinach, cooked, squeezed dry, and chopped
4 tbsp butter
1 cup (250 g) ricotta cheese
Ground nutmeg
Salt and pepper

▪ Sauté cooked, chopped spinach in butter. Allow to cool slightly, then mix with ricotta cheese and pinch of ground nutmeg. Season mixture to taste with salt and pepper. Let cool before using to fill shapes such as tortellini or lunette.

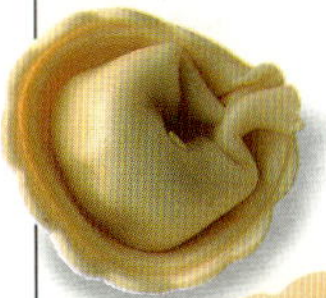

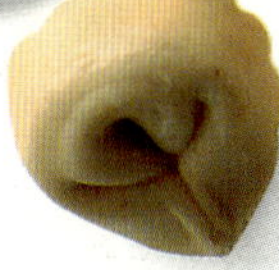

LUNETTE

TORTELLINI

84 SPINACH & CHEESE PINWHEELS

Serves 6 as main course

Ingredients

1 lb (500 g) Fresh egg pasta dough
(see p.20)

Spinach filling
1 lb (500 g) frozen leaf spinach
1 cup (225 g) fresh goat cheese
2 tbsp butter
1 cup (225 g) ricotta cheese
Ground nutmeg
2 eggs, lightly beaten
Salt and pepper

Topping
4 tbsp butter
4 tbsp heavy cream

Red pepper sauce
3 large red peppers
Small bunch fresh basil
2 tbsp olive oil
2 large tomatoes, peeled, seeded, and chopped
1 garlic clove, chopped
2 scallions, chopped

1 Knead and roll out pasta dough; allow to dry until leathery. Cut dough into 4 x 8 in (10 x 20 cm) rectangles. Spread on towel; sprinkle with a little flour. Allow to dry 1–2 hours. Meanwhile cook spinach, drain thoroughly, and squeeze with hands to remove excess moisture. With knife, finely chop spinach. Crumble goat cheese, discarding any rind.

2 Gently melt butter in skillet; add spinach; cook until all moisture has evaporated. Allow to cool slightly, then stir in ricotta and goat cheese, pinch of nutmeg, and salt and pepper to taste. Add eggs and mix well. Cook pasta rectangles in boiling salted water until barely tender. Drain, place in bowl of cold water, then drain again thoroughly.

3 Preheat oven to 375° F/190° C. Spread 3–4 tbsp spinach filling on each pasta rectangle, leaving narrow border. Roll rectangles up from short end and arrange in buttered baking dish. For topping, melt butter, mix with heavy cream, and pour over rolls. Cover baking dish with buttered foil and bake in preheated oven until skewer inserted in pasta roll in center of dish is hot to touch when removed, about 30 minutes.

4 Broil whole red peppers on rack about 4 in (10 cm) from heat, until skin is black and blistered. Place in plastic bag, close, and leave until peppers are cool enough to handle. With table knife, peel skin; remove core; halve each pepper and scrape away seeds. Rinse under running water and pat dry. Cut into chunks. Chop basil leaves, reserving a few sprigs.

5 Heat olive oil in skillet; add roast pepper chunks, chopped tomatoes, garlic, scallions, and basil. Cook until mixture thickens; stir occasionally. Puree sauce in processor until almost smooth. Season with salt and pepper.

TO SERVE

Cut rolls diagonally into slices. Spoon some sauce onto each plate; arrange pinwheels on top. Garnish with reserved basil sprigs.

85 CHEESE TORTELLINI WITH SMOKED SALMON

Serves 6–8 as appetizer or main course

Ingredients

Filling

5 oz (150 g) mozzarella cheese
1¼ cups (300 g) ricotta cheese
⅓ cup (30 g) grated Parmesan cheese
Ground nutmeg
Salt and pepper
1 egg

Topping

¼ lb (125 g) smoked salmon
Small bunch fresh dill
4 tbsp butter
1 cup (250 ml) heavy cream

1 lb (500 g) Fresh egg pasta dough
(see p.20)

1 Cut mozzarella cheese into cubes and place in large bowl. Add ricotta cheese and grated Parmesan cheese and mix well. Add pinch of ground nutmeg and season to taste with salt and pepper.

2 Lightly beat egg and combine with cheeses in bowl. Cut smoked salmon into strips. Chop dill, reserving few sprigs for garnish. Roll out dough and cut into rounds with 2½ in (6 cm) pastry cutter.

3 Using pastry brush or fingers, lightly moisten edge of each pasta round with water. Place 1 teaspoonful cheese filling onto center of each round. Fold one side over to enclose filling. Pinch edges together with fingers. Gently curve around finger, turning sealed edge up to form upward-curved pleat.

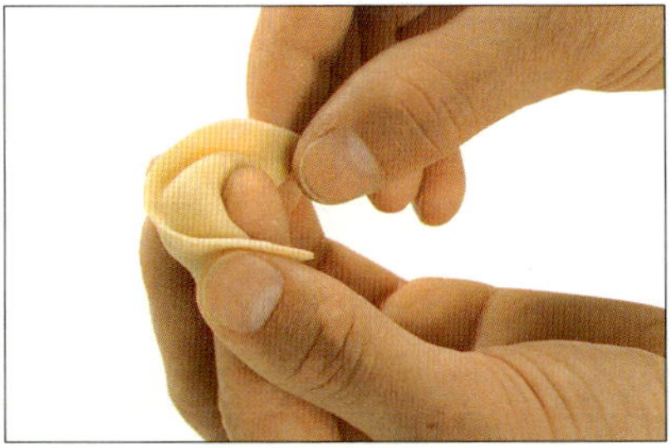

4 Pinch together pointed ends of filled pasta round to form ring. Stuff, seal, and shape remaining pasta dough rounds. Spread out completed tortellini on floured towel and sprinkle lightly with flour or fine cornmeal. Allow to dry 1–2 hours.

5 Cook tortellini in boiling salted water until tender but still chewy, stirring occasionally to prevent sticking. Drain in colander, rinse with hot water, and drain again thoroughly. Meanwhile, gently heat butter in saucepan until melted.

6 Add tortellini to saucepan and gently toss until all are evenly coated with butter. Add cream, smoked salmon, and chopped dill. Toss over moderate heat until ingredients are thoroughly heated.

TO SERVE

Serve tortellini on warmed serving dish and garnish with reserved sprigs of dill.

86 PREVENT TORTELLINI FROM BURSTING

To prevent filled pasta such as tortellini bursting while they are cooking, be careful not to overfill the pasta rounds. Seal the edges of each piece by first moistening with water, then pinching together.

87 EGGPLANT LASAGNE WITH CHEESE SAUCE

Serves 8 as main course

Ingredients

Spinach pasta dough

3 cups (90 g) fresh spinach, cooked, drained, squeezed dry, and finely chopped

2½ cups (300 g) flour

3 eggs

1 tbsp vegetable oil

1 tsp salt

Oil for baking dish

Filling

1 lb (500 g) eggplant

Vegetable oil for brushing eggplant

2 large tomatoes

½ lb (250 g) mozzarella cheese

Cheese sauce

1 quart (1 liter) milk

6 tbsp butter

3 tbsp flour

Ground nutmeg

Salt and pepper

1⅓ cups (125 g) grated Parmesan cheese

1 Make pasta dough *(see p.20)*, adding spinach along with eggs, oil, and salt. Knead and roll out dough, then allow to dry 5–10 minutes. Cut dough into 4 x 8 in (10 x 20 cm) rectangles; spread on floured towel and sprinkle with flour; allow to dry 1–2 hours. Cook in boiling salted water until barely tender, 3–5 minutes. Transfer pasta to bowl of cold water to stop it cooking; remove with slotted spoon and drain thoroughly on clean towel.

2 Trim eggplants; slice thickly. Place in colander, sprinkle with salt, and leave 30 minutes to draw out juices. Heat oven to 350° F/180° C. Rinse eggplant slices and pat dry with paper towel. Place on oiled baking sheets and brush with oil. Bake in preheated oven until tender, turning once, 20–25 minutes. Core and slice tomatoes. Cut mozzarella cheese into ¼ in (5 mm) thick slices.

3 Scald milk in medium saucepan. Melt butter in another pan; whisk in flour and cook for 1–2 minutes. Remove from heat and whisk in scalded milk. Return to heat and cook, whisking, until sauce boils and thickens. Season sauce with pinch of nutmeg and salt and pepper; simmer for 2 minutes. Remove from heat and stir in three-quarters of Parmesan cheese.

4 Preheat oven to 350° F/180° C. Oil 9 x 13 in (23 x 33 cm) baking dish. Cover bottom with layer of cheese sauce, then top with layer of pasta. Arrange half of eggplant slices on top; cover with sauce then another layer of pasta. Place half of mozzarella slices on top of pasta then half of tomato slices. Cover with another layer of pasta topped with eggplant slices.

5 Spoon on another layer of cheese sauce; top with pasta, another layer of mozzarella cheese and tomato slices, and cover all with thick final layer of cheese sauce. Sprinkle with remaining Parmesan cheese and bake in oven 30–45 minutes.

To Serve

When lasagne is bubbling and brown, cut into eight pieces and serve on warm plates.

88 LASAGNE BOLOGNESE

Serves 6–8 as main course

Ingredients

Bolognese sauce
3 large tomatoes
2 tbsp finely chopped onion
2 tbsp finely chopped carrot
2 tbsp finely chopped celery
3 tbsp olive oil
3 tbsp butter
1 lb (500 g) ground beef
1 cup (250 ml) white wine
½ cup (125 ml) milk
Ground nutmeg
Salt and pepper

1 lb (500 g) Fresh egg pasta dough (see p.20)
1 quart (1 liter) Classic béchamel sauce (see p.41)
Freshly grated Parmesan cheese
2 tbsp butter

- Make Bolognese sauce: seed and coarsely chop tomatoes. Sauté onion, carrot, and celery in olive oil and butter till soft. Add ground beef and cook, stirring, until meat loses pink color. Add wine; cook over medium heat until liquid evaporates. Pour in milk with pinch of nutmeg and cook till liquid evaporates. Stir in chopped tomatoes, with their juice. Simmer 3–4 hours, stirring occasionally. Season to taste at end of cooking time.
- Knead and roll out pasta dough; allow to dry 5–10 minutes. Cut dough into 4 x 8 in (10 x 20 cm) rectangles. Spread on floured towel, sprinkle with flour, and allow to dry 1–2 hours.
- Preheat oven to 350° F/180° C. Butter 9 x 13 in (23 x 33 cm) baking dish. Cook pasta in boiling salted water until just tender. Transfer to bowl of cold water, then drain thoroughly.
- Spoon layer of Bolognese sauce over bottom of baking dish followed by layer of Béchamel sauce, sprinkled with Parmesan cheese. Top with layer of pasta rectangles then spread another layer of Bolognese sauce, topped with pasta. Spoon over another layer of Béchamel sauce, then sprinkle with more freshly grated Parmesan cheese.
- Continue layering until dish is nearly full. Finish with layer of Bolognese sauce topped with final thick layer of Béchamel sauce and sprinkling of Parmesan cheese. Dot top with butter. Bake until very hot and top is golden brown and bubbling, 30-40 minutes.
- Allow to rest for 5 minutes before cutting. Serve on warmed plates.

89 MACARONI WITH FENNEL & RAISINS

Serves 4–6 as main course

Ingredients

1 lb (500 g) fennel bulbs
Salt and pepper
⅜ cup (45 g) pine nuts
2 medium onions, thinly sliced
½ cup (125 ml) olive oil
¼ cup (45 g) raisins
2 cups (500 g) ricotta cheese
4 cups (375 g) macaroni
½ lb (250 g) mozzarella cheese, sliced

TO SERVE
Serve macaroni on warmed plates. If you like, garnish with chopped fennel leaves.

▪ Trim fennel bulbs; cut lengthwise in half, then slice crosswise. Cook in boiling salted water until just tender. Drain, reserving cooking liquid. Allow to cool then chop coarsely. Preheat oven to 375° F/190° C; spread out pine nuts on baking sheet; bake until golden brown.

▪ In skillet, sauté onions in oil until soft; add fennel, raisins, and pine nuts and stir. Take pan off heat and, when mixture is cool, stir in ricotta.

▪ In large pan, bring fennel cooking liquid, plus extra water if required, to boil; cook macaroni and drain. Preheat oven to 350 °F/180° C.

▪ Place half of macaroni in buttered baking dish; top with half of ricotta mixture. Repeat layers of macaroni and ricotta topping. Place mozzarella cheese slices evenly over top of macaroni. Bake until cheese is melted and golden brown, and macaroni is very hot, 15–20 minutes.

90 RAVIOLI WITH SAFFRON RICOTTA

Serves 4 as main course

Ingredients

1 lb (500 g) Fresh egg pasta dough (see p.20)
¼ tsp saffron
1 tbsp milk
1½ cups (375 g) ricotta cheese
Grated zest of 1 orange
1 egg
Nutmeg
Salt and pepper
½ cup (125 g) butter
Sage or rosemary leaves

- Make dough and allow to rest for 1 hour. Divide dough in two and roll out thinly into two rectangles of equal size. Soak saffron in milk for 20 minutes, then mix into ricotta, along with orange zest, lightly beaten egg, pinch of grated nutmeg, and salt and pepper to taste. Place teaspoonfuls of ricotta stuffing on one sheet of pasta, in rows approximately 1½ in (3.5 cm) apart.
- Place second pasta rectangle on top and press down lightly with fingers between rows of filling. Cut between rows with pastry wheel or sharp knife to form squares of ravioli. Press firmly with fingertips around edges of ravioli, making certain that they are well sealed. Allow to dry on floured towel for 1–2 hours.
- Bring large pan of salted water to boil. Cook ravioli until they puff up slightly, 5 minutes. Meanwhile, melt butter and flavor with whole sage or chopped rosemary leaves.
- Drain ravioli carefully and toss in flavored butter until well coated.

91 DELICATE PASTAS

Small filled pastas, such as ravioli and tortellini, are delicate to work with. To help prevent them from breaking or sticking to each other during cooking, freeze them first: after filling, dry for 1 hour, then lay in single layer on a floured baking sheet. Freeze until solid, about 1 hour, then cook as directed.

DRY ON FLOURED SURFACE

92 CANNELLONI WITH CHICKEN & PANCETTA

Serves 6–8 as main course

Ingredients

1 lb (500 g) Fresh egg pasta dough (see p.20)
2⅔ cups (375 g) cooked chicken breast, shredded
¼ lb (125 g) mozzarella cheese, cubed
2 eggs, lightly beaten
Salt and pepper
6 thin slices pancetta

1½ cups (375 ml) Fresh tomato sauce (see p.41)
2 tbsp chopped fresh basil leaves
⅓ cup (30 g) grated Parmesan cheese

- Roll out dough thinly; trim edges and cut into 4 x 3 in (10 x 7.5 cm) rectangles. Spread out on towel and sprinkle with flour. Allow to dry 1–2 hours. Cook pasta rectangles in boiling salted water until barely tender, stirring gently to prevent sticking. Transfer to bowl of cold water. Remove and drain thoroughly on towel.
- Place chicken, mozzarella cubes, and eggs in bowl. Add salt and pepper to taste. Mix well.
- Preheat oven to 400° F/200° C. Cut each slice of pancetta into four strips, discarding any bone or rind. Place one strip on each rectangle. Place 2–3 tablespoons filling onto each rectangle, along one long edge. Butter or oil large baking dish. Roll up each rectangle into a cylinder and arrange in baking dish, seam side down.
- Add basil to tomato sauce and spoon over cannelloni in baking dish. Bake in heated oven until bubbling, 20–25 minutes.

TO SERVE

Sprinkle with Parmesan cheese and, if you like, garnish with basil leaves.

93 BAKED RIGATONI WITH MEATBALLS

Serves 6–8 as main course

Ingredients

3 lb (1.4 kg) fresh plum tomatoes, peeled, seeded, and chopped
3 garlic cloves, finely chopped
Medium bunch fresh basil, chopped
Salt and pepper

Meatballs
1 lb (500 g) lean ground beef
1⅓ cups (125 g) grated Parmesan cheese
3–5 sprigs flat-leaf parsley, chopped
Juice of ½ lemon
Salt and pepper
1 egg
3 tbsp olive oil, plus more for soufflé dish

¾ lb (375 g) rigatoni

1 Put tomatoes, with any juice, in skillet with two-thirds of chopped garlic and basil leaves. Cook over medium heat until mixture is slightly thickened, 10–12 minutes, stirring occasionally. Transfer mixture to food processor and process till smooth. Season to taste with salt and pepper; set aside. Wipe skillet clean.

2 Put beef, quarter of Parmesan cheese, parsley, remaining garlic, lemon juice, and salt and pepper in bowl. Add egg and mix well. With wet hands, shape into balls ¾ in (2 cm) in diameter. Heat olive oil in skillet and fry meatballs briskly, turning with knife, until brown on outside and still pink inside, 2–4 minutes. Transfer to large plate.

CHECK DONENESS

FRY IN BATCHES

3 Preheat oven to 375° F/190° C. Brush inside of 2 quart (2 liter) soufflé dish with oil. Cook pasta in boiling salted water until *al dente*, 8–10 minutes, stirring occasionally to prevent sticking. Drain thoroughly. Return pasta to pan and pour in tomato-basil sauce. Toss pasta and sauce together until pasta is well coated.

4 Spoon about one-third of rigatoni and sauce mixture into soufflé dish and level surface. Place half of fried meatballs on top. Sprinkle with about 1 tablespoon Parmesan cheese. Add half of remaining pasta and sauce, then rest of meatballs.

5 Sprinkle top with another tablespoon of Parmesan. Add rest of pasta and cover with remainder of Parmesan cheese. Bake in oven until very hot and top is browned, 30–40 minutes. Allow to stand until flavors blend, about 15 minutes.

TO SERVE

Sprinkle with grated Parmesan cheese; if you like, garnish with shredded basil.

94 CHINESE MOONS WITH LEMON SAUCE

Serves 8–10 as appetizer

Ingredients

6 oz (175 g) peeled cooked shrimp
¼ lb (125 g) napa cabbage
1 lemon
1 in (2.5 cm) piece fresh ginger root
1 tbsp vegetable oil
1 garlic clove, chopped
1 shallot, chopped
1 tsp sherry
1 tbsp soy sauce

1 lb (500 g) Fresh egg pasta dough
(see p.20)

Lemon sauce
2 lemons
3 tsbp butter
5 tbsp heavy cream

1 Prepare shrimp filling: coarsely chop shrimp; set aside. With sharp knife, remove core of napa cabbage and finely shred leaves. Discard any thick ribs. Rinse leaves under running cold water. Bring pan of salted water to boil, add napa cabbage, and simmer until barely tender. Drain in colander, rinse with cold water, and drain again thoroughly. Grate zest from lemon with fine grater; set aside.

2 Peel and finely chop ginger root. Heat oil in frying pan and add shredded napa cabbage, chopped garlic, shallot, and ginger. Sauté mixture for about 3 minutes, stirring frequently. Add shrimp, lemon zest, sherry, and soy sauce and stir well. Taste filling to check seasoning. Process mixture in food processor until coarsely chopped or, if you prefer, chop finely with sharp knife.

3 On floured surface, knead and roll out pasta dough to thickness of postcard. With pastry cutter, cut out 3 in (7.5 cm) rounds. Spoon 1 teaspoonful filling onto center of each round. Lightly brush around edge with water. Fold one side of pasta round over to enclose filling. Seal carefully by pinching edges together securely with fingertips. Repeat filling and sealing with all remaining dough rounds.

4 Spread filled pasta moons on floured towel; sprinkle with flour. Allow to dry 1–2 hours. Meanwhile, prepare lemon sauce: grate zest from lemons, using finest side of grater. Melt butter in small pan; add heavy cream and half of lemon zest; stir. Keep warm while cooking pasta moons.

5 Cook pasta moons in boiling salted water until edges are tender but still chewy, 2–3 minutes. Stir occasionally to prevent sticking. Drain in colander, rinse with hot water, then drain thoroughly. Arrange on warmed individual plates.

TO SERVE

Spoon lemon sauce over pasta moons and sprinkle with lemon zest. If you like, add some finely sliced green scallion.

Store & Reheat Pasta

95 Store dry pasta

Thoroughly dry homemade pasta; sprinkle with flour and keep in an airtight container for three to four days (egg pasta) or up to one week (eggless pasta). Store-bought dried pasta will last for about two years.

Airtight Jars
Store dried pasta in sealed jars in a cool, dry place.

96 Fresh pasta storage

Place homemade filled pasta on a baking sheet, dust lightly with flour, and refrigerate for up to one day. Or open-freeze on a tray, pack in plastic bags, and freeze for two months. Follow maker's guidelines for storing store-bought fresh pasta.

FREEZE FILLED PASTA

97 Prepare & store pasta salad

Whether intended as a side salad or appetizer, or a substantial main-course meal, a pasta salad can be made up to one day ahead. Toss the ingredients and dressing while the pasta is warm so that it absorbs the flavorings fully. Cover the salad and store in the refrigerator until needed. Serve chilled, or bring to room temperature before serving.

98 FREEZE SAUCES

Pasta sauces that are based on cream, milk, or cheese do not freeze well, since such ingredients will tend to separate when frozen. Tomato sauces, on the other hand, freeze particularly well, as do Pesto and Ragù Bolognese. Filled and layered pasta dishes that incorporate sauces, such as lasagne, will also freeze and reheat satisfactorily.

FREEZE SAUCE IN PLASTIC BAG

99 DEFROST WELL

Defrost frozen pasta sauces and prepared pasta dishes at room temperature or, more slowly, in the refrigerator. Alternatively, you can use a microwave oven to speed up the process, following the guidelines supplied with your particular oven.

100 REFRIGERATE

If you wish to prepare a pasta sauce ahead of time, or have some sauce left over, store it in an airtight container in the refrigerator for up to one day. Uncooked, filled pasta, such as ravioli, can also be kept in the refrigerator for one day.

101 REHEAT PASTA

Reheat, until bubbling, pasta sauces that have been stored in the refrigerator or frozen then defrosted. Stir gently to ensure that the ingredients are mixed. Layered pasta dishes reheat very well in a microwave oven.

REHEAT LAYERED PASTA
You can prepare layered pasta dishes up to 24 hours ahead. Keep refrigerated and bake conventionally, or in a microwave oven, when needed.

INDEX

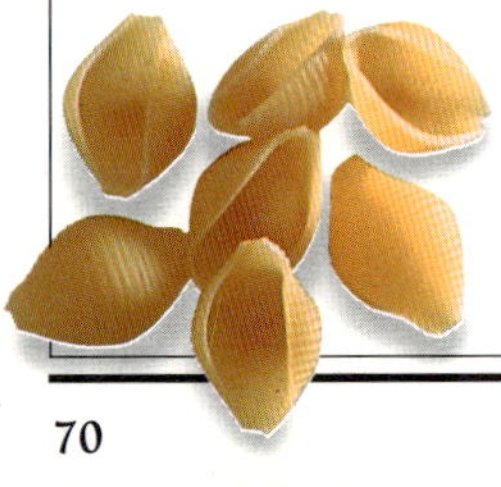

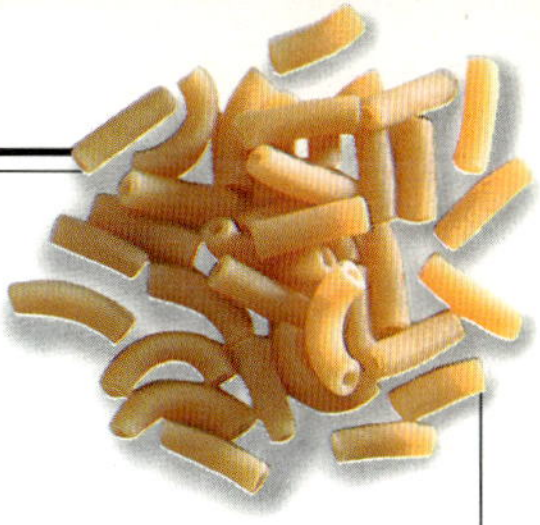

Acknowledgments

Dorling Kindersley would like to thank Chris Benton for recipe conversions, Hilary Bird for compiling the index, Ann Kay for proofreading, Murdo Culver for design assistance, Bella Pringle and Alexa Stace for editorial assistance, and Mark Bracey for computer assistance.

Photography

KEY: t *top*; b *bottom*; c *center*; l *left*; r *right*

All photography by Amanda Heywood, David Murray, and Clive Streeter except for:
Martin Brigdale 42 all except cl; Philip Dowell 10tr, br; 11tr, br; 12tr, tl; 32tr, cr; 61tr; 62cl, c; Stephen Oliver 32br; Roger Phillips 8bl; 12c, bl, bc, br; 16br, bl, cr; 2tr; 53; Susanna Price 30br; Matthew Ward 7; 28bl; 68; 69tr; Jerry Young 25tr; 26 all except tr.

The recipe on page 62 originally appeared in *Little Library Pasta* by Jill Norman (Dorling Kindersley 1990).